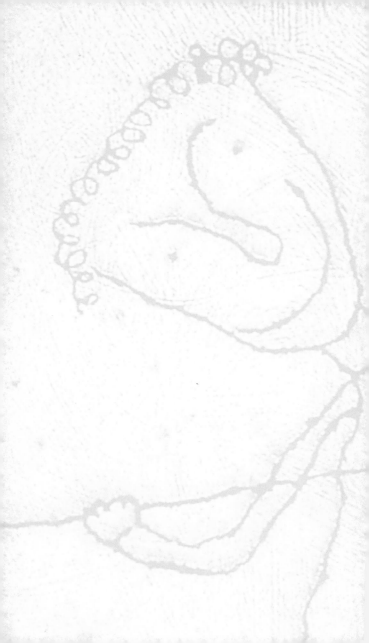

Tiny Boat

God bless this tiny little boat
And me who travels in it;
It stays afloat for years and years
And sinks within a minute.

And so the soul in which we sail
Unknown by years of thinking
Is deeply felt and understood
The minute that it's sinking.

A Little Duck

With a bit of luck
A duck
Will come into your life.

When you are at the peak
Of your great powers,
And your achievement towers
Like a smoking chimney stack,
There'll be a quack
And right there at your feet
A little duck will stand;
She will take you by the hand
And lead you

Like a child with no defence;
She will lead you
Into wisdom, joy and innocence.
That little duck.

I wish you luck.

True Happiness

How may a man measure his own happiness?
He must first go to his cupboard
   and take out all his neckties.
Then he must lay them out on the ground
End to end.
Then he must measure the length of this
   line of neckties,
And that measurement,
That distance,
Is exactly the same as his distance from
   true happiness.

A Book

On the armchair, a book:
How to Relax.
Beside the bed, a book:
How to Get to Sleep.
Next to the window, a book:
How to See What's in Front of You.
Next to the man, a book:
How to be a Man.
On the desk, a book:
How to Succeed in Life.
In hell, a book:
How You Ended up in Hell.

No Sooner

No sooner do you arrive than it's
   time to leave.
How beautiful it is, how glorious,
Yet it's nearly time to go.
So you take it in, you take it in.

And you take a few small souvenirs,
Some leaves: lavender, rosemary,
   eucalyptus;
A few small pebbles, a few small secrets,
A look you received, nine little notes
   of music,
And then it's time to go.

You move towards the open door
And the silent night beyond,

The few bright stars, a deep breath,
And it really is time to go.

No sooner does it all begin to make sense
Does it start to come true,
Does it all open up,
Do you begin to see,
Does it enter into your heart ...
No sooner do you arrive than it's time
    to leave.

Yes, it's the truth.
And then you will have passed through it,
And with mysterious consequence
It will have passed through you.

A Dusty Little Swag

All my father left me
Was a dusty little swag
And a pair of tiny booties
In a crumpled paper bag,
And he left me in confusion
And he left me in despair
And he left the swag and booties
For the walk to God knows where.

Let It Go

Let it go,

Let it out,

Let it all unravel;

Let it free

And it will be

A path on which to travel.

At the Top

At the top of the tallest building
  in the world
Sat the saddest man in the world
And inside the man
Was the loneliest heart in the world
And inside the heart
Was the deepest pit in the world
And at the bottom of the pit
Was the blackest mud in the world
And in the mud lay the lightest,
  loveliest, tenderest,
Most beautiful, happy angel in
  the universe.

Autumn

Leaves are falling and revealing
One of winter's eerie sights:
On the trees, how unappealing,
Wire for the fairy lights.

Wire with plastic insulation
Stapled onto every limb;
Circuits in the vegetation
Indicate that life is grim.

Misery in any city
Can be measured, if you please,
By counting with the eye of pity
Fairy lights installed in trees.

Magpie

Magpie, magpie, dive on me,
Swoop down from your holy tree;
As I pass the flower bed
Stick your beak into my head.

Magpie, magpie, make a hole,
Through my head into my soul;
As I pass beneath the sun
Bring my troubled head undone.

Magpie, magpie, it is spring,
Is my soul a happy thing?
As I pass around the tree
Make a hole so you can see.

Hair

We give thanks for the mystery of hair:
Too little here and too much there,
Censored and shaved, controlled and
  suppressed,
Unwelcome guest in soups and sandwiches,
Difficult growth always needing attention,
Gentle and comforting, complex and wild,
Reminding us softly that we might
  be animals,
Growing and growing 'til the day that
  we die
And the day after as well, so they say.

In all of its places, in all of its ways,
We give thanks for the blessing of hair.

Common Sense

Cross my heart, I remember
When common sense was delivered to
  the door
Each morning by horse and cart,
Equally to the rich and poor.

What a bold start it was
To find it sitting there on the porch,
All yours, fresh as a daisy
And as good as gold.

Completely undebated was common sense;
Unprocessed, you might say,
Full of organisms and rough seeds.
It's what the body needs.
You could feel it do you good.

How could
Such a useful thing,

So plentiful back then
Yet so revered,
Become so lost and rare
And so weird?

You have to go through so much
  these days,
Crawl across a field of broken bottles,
Half a life of suffering and sin,
Be done over and done in
Before you find it once again.

Perhaps one morning
On the porch
And in the sun of early spring,
Lo and behold,
On the step, thank Christ,
A little common sense is there again.

A Winter's Poem

A clever creature is the snake,
Who spends his winter not awake;
He snuggles in his long thin bed
And brews up venom in this head.

The human is a different sort;
He spends the winter watching sport;
He yells abuse in concrete stands
And empties out his poison glands.

Upon the Sagging Mattress

Upon the sagging mattress known as life
The weary husband lays down with
  his wife
To feel the nasty shapes and awful lumps
To get no rest, to only get the grumps.

And yet upon this drooping bag of woe
They close their eyes and sometimes
  have a go
At fantasising sweeter, better things:
A life with good support and inner springs.

Duck Study

How you will know
If a person,
Perhaps a politician, a policeman,
A partner or a priest,
Is corrupt:

You must study the duck.
You must play with the duck.
You must talk with the duck.
You must know the ways of the duck.
You must look deeply into the eyes
   of the duck.
Then, looking into the face of the person,
How will you know if that person
   is corrupt?
You will know.
YOU WILL KNOW.

The Inner Horse

You can lead a horse to water
But you can't make it cheerful;
The bucket is full
But the horse is tearful,
So you give it a loving earful:
'What's up, old fellah?' you say.
He looks at you and looks away.
Of course.
The dear old inner horse.

He Was a Man

In Menswear
He shot a brightly coloured sportscoat
With his trusty bow.

He harpooned
A large, fat couch
In the furniture department.

He clubbed
A pop-up toaster
In the electrical section.

With his bare hands
He fought a king-size quilt
In Bedding.

He cast his net in Footwear

And caught

A magnificent pair of slippers.

He was a hunter.

He was a provider.

He was a MAN.

Here I Am (manifesto)

Here I am,
Alive on earth.
Conscious,
Unconscious,
Semi-conscious.
Knowing others,
Known to others,
Yet also unknowable
And alone forever.
Soon I will not be here.
Hurrah!

How to Get There

Go to the end of the path until you get
    to the gate.

Go through the gate and head straight
    out towards the horizon.

Keep going towards the horizon.

Sit down and have a rest every now
    and again,
But keep on going, just keep on with it.

Keep on going as far as you can.

That's how you get there.

How to Hold Onto It

Hold onto it like you hold a day-old
  chicken.
Hold onto it like you hold a live fish.
Hold onto it like you hold a horse.
Hold onto it like you hold a bowl of soup.
Hold onto it like you hold a door open
  for the Queen Mother.
Letting go of it is just as difficult
And shall be dealt with at some later stage.

Ceremony

We are gathered here
To witness the marriage
Of Fiona and Simon.

Simon, do you accept
That you are a complete jerk?
'I do.'

And do you, Fiona, accept
That you are an absolute bitch?
'I do.'

I now declare you married
In the full sense.
Congratulations.

A Biography

He took it like a man
Right on the chin,
And when he was older
His jaw caved in.

She took it politely
With a sweet smile,
But when she was older
She was thoroughly vile.

They took their revenge
And got very rich,
The chinless wonder
And the vile old bitch.

Homes Are Quietly Burning

Homes are quietly burning,
Madness on the march,
Lies move unresisted through the land.
We stand helpless as our lives are occupied
Faster than we understand.
Collaborators wave their little flags
As ugliness takes over.
'Make a friend of ugliness,' they say.
'Learn the language, then you won't
   get hurt.'

But you will,
No matter how you crawl.
A knock on the door one night,
A scuffle in the hall,
Your heart rubbed in the dirt.
'All right!' you scream your indecision,
'Take the children but leave the television.'

So you stand by useless
As childhood is trashed,
Innocence reviled,
The truth is bashed.
The home and the idea of home
Is set on fire, and still you stand by
As the goodness in your culture burns.
You stand there in the glow,
Going, going,
Going with the flow.

Ah yes, the flow. Heaven help us!

One day you might be asked,
'How come you didn't know what was
    going on?
Why did you not fight?'
'Fight?' you'll say. 'That's a word that
    never occurred.'

The very word brings tears.
It will dawn on you after all those
  painful years
That to fight is one of the most beautiful,
  simple, and useful ideas.

Literature

The pen is mightier than the sword
And mightier than the literary award;
Without the pen we'd be unable
To leave those notes on the kitchen table:
Nothing lovelier ever penned,
With three small crosses at the end,
Made for no one else to see,
The literature of you and me.

Little Tendrils

Little tendrils of the heart
Curling out and groping,
Seeking little things to hold,
Wiggling and hoping.

Little tendrils of the soul
Delicate and perky,
Seeking little surfaces
Peculiar and quirky.

Little tendrils, little tendrils,
Innocent and plucky,
I pray that you are careful
And I hope that you are lucky.

Scraps

Little scraps of peace and quiet,
Hope, conversation, handshakes –
All in dribs and drabs.
A few crumbs of fun,
A tiny flake of beauty,
One teaspoon of enthusiasm –
Offcuts of each other.
A skerrick of community,
A bit of a kiss.
A snippet of eye contact,
A snippet of hospitality,
A snippet of patience,
A shred of honour,
A wisp of good humour,
A sample of compassion –

Leftovers, oddments,

Remnants of the glorious situation.

A fragment of God,

Not much, really.

Sorry, time's up.

Love is Born

Love is born
With a dark and troubled face,
When hope is dead
And in the most unlikely place;
Love is born,
Love is always born.

The Bottle

I met a man perched on a bottle
With a woman deep inside,
Rising slowly up towards him,
Floating on the tears he cried.

Said he, 'It's only tears can save her,
Tears of sorrow, tears of pain.
I'm going to have to feel a lot,
Until I have her back again.'

All sniffling and snuffling,
He said, 'It almost makes me laugh
To think that if you weep enough
A man can find his better half.'

Us

Last night while looking at the sky
I saw a little planet die.
It died and fell without a fuss;
I wondered whether it was us,
Or part of us that I had seen
Disintegrate. It could have been.

Mother Earth

Poor old lonely mother earth
Is very, very sad;
She had a bomb put in her heart
By people who are mad.
She held them and she fed them,
She taught them to be free;
They put a bomb inside her heart
And whispered, *'C'est la vie.'*

Modern Stupid

It's much easier
To be stupid these days
Than in previous times.

Back in the old days
They had to do it all by hand.
It was sheer drudgery.

Now we can do it faster
And with more comfort,
Thanks to modern methods.

You can fit it into a busy life,
It's available to everyone.
It's right there at your fingertips.

My Big Toe

My big toe is an honest man,
So down to earth and normal,
Always true unto himself
And pleasantly informal.
Full of simple energy,
Contented with his role.
If all of me could be like him
I'd be a happy soul.

Ode to Her Majesty

I did but see her passing by, she passed
   me by quite fast.
I saw her passing by again when several
   years had passed.
And then at some much later stage she
   passed me by once more
And there were further passings-by
   and these I also saw.
I did but see her passing by, I don't
   know what it means;
Perhaps it's not my problem, but
   a problem of the Queen's.

Mr Rabbit

Mr Rabbit came to Australia with his wife
To raise a family and make a brand
   new life.
'Let us rejoice for we are young and free,'
He said while touching Mrs Rabbit on
   the knee.
They rushed ashore and quickly dug a hole,
Then lay down side by side and lost
   control.

My Shoe

Since I hurt my pendulum
My life is all erratic,
My parrot who was cordial
Is now transmitting static.
The carpet died, a palm collapsed,
The cat keeps doing poo;
The only thing that keeps me sane
Is talking to my shoe.

Our Father

A spectacular event
Which suddenly surpasses
The great news stories of the world:

Our father,
Normally a worried and serious man,
Does an underwater handstand
In the bay.

Peace

Peace is my drug;
It stops the pain.
In safe reflecting rooms
Or in a lane,
Or in a park,
I will lie
And have some peace
And get high.

If it's pure
And there's a lot of it about
I overdose
And pass out
And dream of peace:
My favourite thing
When nobody wants me
And nothing's happening.

Artist, Leave
the World of Art

Artist, leave the world of art,
Pack your goodies on a cart,
Duck out through some tiny hole,
Slip away and save your soul.

Leave no footprints, don't look back,
Take the dark and dirty track.
Cross the border, cross your heart:
Freedom from the world of art.

Anthem

Underpants which have in winter sagged
And fallen into darkness and despond
Shall from their shame and loneliness
  be dragged
And laid upon the fern's emerging frond.
The frond shall gently rise to greet
  the spring,
Above the flowers into the sun fantastic,
Where birds in praise of underpants
  shall sing
And life shall be restored to old elastic.
Yes, life shall be restored to old elastic.

Sitting on the Fence

Come sit down beside me,
I said to myself,
And although it doesn't make sense,
I held my own hand
As a small sign of trust
And together I sat on the fence.

Moments of no Consequence

Moments of no consequence
Seem to make a lot of sense,
Like the gentle pitter-patter
Of the things that do not matter,
As I sit alone and stare,
Neither here and neither there.

Such a Fuss

Each day — such a fuss,
Such praise, such damnation:
Ooh, ahh, yes, no ...!
Exhaustion and disintegration.

Such a fuss, yet the goat
Eats little flowers and thorns
And hears the sparrow
Singing brightly in his horns
(The sun is sweet, the afternoon
　lies sleeping in the valley),
A song for little flowers and thorns
Digesting in the belly.

The Awfulisers

Every night and every day
The awfulisers work away,
Awfulising public places,
Favourite things and little graces;
Awfulising lovely treasures,
Common joys and simple pleasures;
Awfulising far and near
The parts of life we held so dear:
Democratic, clean and lawful,
Awful, awful, awful, awful.

The Empty Jeff

An empty Jeff came through the clouds
And hung there for a minute,
A vacuum in the shape of Jeff
With no Jeff in it!

'The empty Jeff, the empty Jeff,'
The people cried in awe,
All staring at the space where Jeff
Was very much no more.

Ode to a Jet-ski Person

Jet-ski person, selfish fink,
May your silly jet-ski sink,
May you hit a pile of rocks,
Oh hoonish, summer, coastal pox.

Noisy, smoking, dickhead fool
On your loathsome leisure tool,
Give us all a jolly lark
And sink beside a hungry shark.

Scream as in its fangs you go,
Your last attention-seeking show,
While on the beach we all join in
With 'Three cheers for the dorsal fin!'

Robin Hood

Robin Hood, Robin Hood,
You'd be napalmed in the wood,
I am very sad to say,
If you were alive today.

Gratitude and Grief

In the cradle of his mother's arms
    a baby lies
Warm and sheltered from the time
    when they will come apart
Gazing from the hidden world into
    his mother's eyes
From where the holy secrets tumble
    down into his heart.

Then with this heart so full of hope
    he travels in the wild
But soon is set upon and cruelly
    beaten to the ground
And wakes upon the ruins of his
    innocence defiled
And there his sacred revelations
    in the mud are found.

Tears of blood and anger flowing
   from his wounded eye
From his violated mouth the song
   of disbelief
In his shattered memory a shattered
   lullaby
But from his broken heart flow
   gratitude and grief.

Woes Maketh the Man

Woes maketh the man.
A troubled heart on a well-cut sleeve,
A well-cut lip, a loose weave,
A sock on the jaw,
A pullover,
A fallover on the floor,
A collar well pressed
Against the wall,
Another cuff, another fall,
A good belt, a black tie,
A black eye, a huge welt,
A felt hat, a hate deeply felt,
A fate with a rip in the rear,
A nicely stitched ear,
A scarf to match the scar,
A scarlet scratch upon the cheek,

A splash of crimson from the nose.

Ah yes,

What maketh the man is his woes.

The Golden Thread

I'm looking for life's precious little
   golden thread.
We've got the rusty chain, the tangled
   wire, the thick rope,
But we can't help you with the golden
   thread, I'm afraid.
What do you want it for?
I want to just see it, I want to smile at it.
I want to tell life's precious little golden
   thread that I love it.
That's all I want.
We've got the ball of string, the reel of
   packaging tape and the optic fibre cable,
But I'm sorry,
We don't have the golden thread any more.

The Home for the Appalled

They took him on a stretcher
To the Home for the Appalled
Where he lay down in a corner
And he bawled and bawled and bawled.

'There's nothing wrong with me,'
  he wailed,
When asked about his bawling,
'It's the world that needs attention;
It's so utterly appalling.'

'It's so utterly appalling,'
He sobbed and cried and bawled,
And the chorus rose to join him
At the Home for the Appalled.

The Crowdless Man

See him wandering alone,
The crowdless man,
He has no group,
He has no tribe,
He carries his identity in his pocket.
His pocket has a hole in it,
His story has a hole in it,
His tragedy is not a tune you can hum.
His suffering and sacrifice,
They have no handles;
His persecution has no logo,
No shrine, no yardstick.
His joy has no credentials,
His observations have no fixed address;
There are no awards whatsoever.

His gaze and yearning are way
  outside the loop,
His pilgrimage has lots of holes in it.
See him wandering alone
Beaming to himself.

The Gentle Hum

I wonder,
Will it all click into place?
I feel it might.
I had a glimpse
That things could all come right.
I'd wake up
On a sunny, slightly roostered morn
And wouldn't realise at first;
The rightness would take time to dawn.
And gradually
The thing would start to gleam;
This worried life I'd had,
This awful world, this painful mess —
It was, in fact, a kind of dream.
The penny would just drop
Into my hand,
The penny that I'd lost so long ago,

And all the peace withheld and blocked
   from me
Would start to flow.
The gentle hum, the gold and silver light
Would all resume;
The fairies and the pixies,
The particles of dust
Caught in the sunlight in my room.
I'd pick up
Where I'd been so rudely interrupted;
I'd have it back again for keeps,
My dog, my brilliant grasp of life,
My backyard and my paddocks full
   of time,
The world all glad around me,
My rightful place,
My joyous leaps.

A Child is a Grub

A child is a grub,
A man's a cocoon,
Music's a butterfly...
Sing me a tune.